Barry Dawson

STREET graphics

india

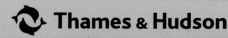

THIS WAY
ईधर से

with 154 illustrations in colour

Thames & Hudson

Dedicated to
Terri Ben, Chote and
Pappu Kapoor

First published in the United
Kingdom in 1999 by Thames &
Hudson Ltd, 181A High
Holborn, London WC1V 7QX

www.thamesandhudson.com

© 1999 Thames & Hudson Ltd,
London

Reprinted 2001

British Library Cataloguing-in-
Publication Data
A catalogue record for this
book is available from the
British Library
ISBN 0-500-28095-9

Printed in Hong Kong
by H & Y Printing Limited

Thanks to
England: Lynne Baxendale, Phil Foster, Grant Devine,
John Gillow, Andy Vaines, Kevin Gabbitas and Ilay Cooper.
H. A. West Photo Suppliers – Leeds, Fuji UK Ltd.

India: Andy and Renu, Mehra family (New Delhi), Kapoor family, Niros Restaurant (Jaipur),
Gangeshwar, Gopal, Rafiq and Ashok, the Rambagh tea-stand rickshaw crew.

Germany: Sibylle Hinterwinkler and Stefan Baggan.

CONTENTS

T

HE STREETS OF INDIA ARE FILLED WITH VIVID
representations of popular cultural themes. These range across political
utopianism, religious celebration and commercial advertising, present-
ing a visual parade of transport, animals and people, hoardings, street furniture,
architectural detail, packaging, display – backdrops and props of a rich cultural street theatre. Striking images blur in a confusion of colour, scale and quantity. Static or moving,
figure or landscape, every surface is a panorama, every material a canvas, an opportunity
for expression and communication. India's hectic festive calendar adds transient decorative
layers of dye, paint, flowers and lights over a continuous celebration of street graphics.

From a simple handprint on a village wall to giant cut-out film stars downtown, tradition is evident in contemporary Indian street graphics. Today, symbols and motifs of an ancient culture provide a diverse visual reference for both traditional and modern applications through equally varied mediums. For example, three-dimensional representations of the Hindu deity Rama, carved in stone, can be found in temples throughout India – centuries-old focal points for religious worship. On auspicious days, rickshaw drivers may spontaneously finger-paint white lines on their vehicle as an abstract representation of Rama. The same deity in full-colour figurative representation can be seen promoting commercial products and services on hoardings.

Most work is hand-rendered. Images are not produced with the uniformity of computer design and lithographic printing, but are individually crafted by street artists with particular and regional variations in style and technique. Trucks, buses and rickshaws are transformed into kinetic art, personalized with symbols and motifs of religious and natural imagery. Sign painters clinging to precarious wooden scaffolds skilfully execute large hoardings, working from memory, sketches or magazine reproductions.

Only
Nothing
is better
than
on County   Casual Wear

RIBUTORS   PULLEPPADI CROSS ROAD   PH: 361924, 311924
             ERNAKULAM, COCHIN-18   312924

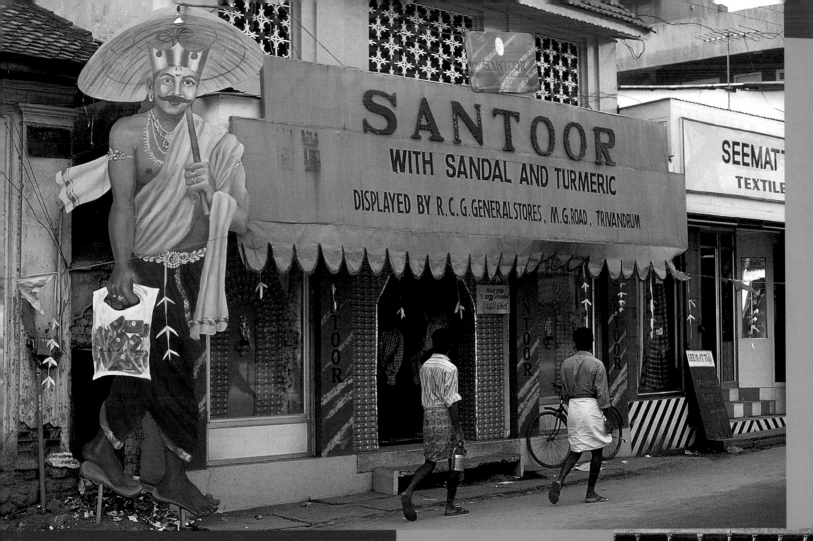

SANTOOR
WITH SANDAL AND TURMERIC
DISPLAYED BY R.C.G.GENERAL STORES, M.G. ROAD, TRIVANDRUM

SEEMATTI
TEXTILE

INTRODUCTION

10

India has traditionally absorbed invading cultures, making them uniquely Indian. Western influence, evident here in turn-of-the-century wall paintings, is fast developing through an expanding market for western goods. Tradition in North Indian street art now contrasts with increasing international image-making, advertising and marketing styles and techniques. The South retains a stronger indigenous influence, resisting the homogeneous while developing and celebrating its own diversity.

The density of India's street imagery generates an overwhelming visual collage. Juxtaposition creates incongruity, humour and irony. A visiting westerner, even with a background of research and experience, reads the imagery using ingrained western cultural

references which differ vastly from the signs and signifiers of Indian cultural reference.

This is a subjective view of street art in India's cities, towns and villages – a personal choice of photographs, isolated from the penetrating aromas, sounds and intense humanity of Indian streets. Selected and ordered clues to a visual influx of chaos, most of these images will have been replaced, added to or altered before publication. This is a document that celebrates the fun of that ephemeral process.

TRANSPORT

12

An Indian-manufactured truck acquires status with a Mercedes logo. Open eyes, representing vigilance, and 'Inshallah' (God willing) painted on the front (in a variety of spellings) indicate a Muslim driver familiar with Indian road hazards.

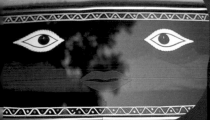

In Mumbai (Bombay), India's commercial centre, the rickshaw is banned and taxicabs proliferate. Rear-window graphics in cut-out adhesive vinyl compete for attention. Main themes include religion, politics, nationalism, cinema and nature.

NEWBOMBAY PANVEL BHAYANDER

SHRADHA

SABURI

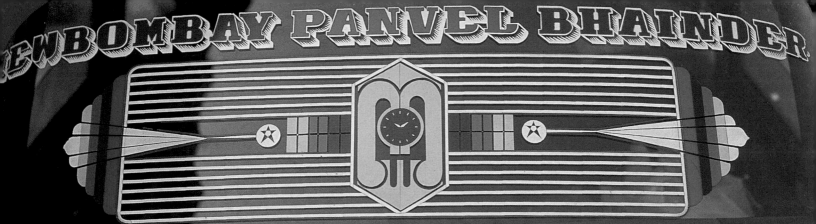

NEWBOMBAY PANVEL BHAINDER

ESSEL WORLD

NEWBOMBAY PANVEL BHAYANDER

QUEEN

THANE

BOMBAY BHAYENDER

THANE

We too! Ours one!

SOUNDHAN

FORD

TMZ 5929

PREMIER TIMBERS MUDICKAC

KEEP YOUR DISTANCE

Kerala's goods trucks are decorated in painted carved wood and pressed metal plate with proverbs, owners' names and warnings to other road users.

TRANSPORT

The majority of Keralan goods trucks feature bold designs painted behind the driver's cab. Images of flora and fauna share popularity with Kerala's three dominant faiths: Christianity, Hinduism and Islam.

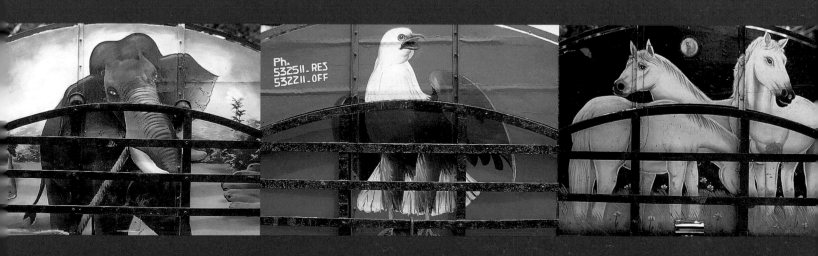

20

TRANSPORT

Painted 'faces' are popular on Tamil Nadu's rickshaws, giving them the appearance of living creatures. Manufacturer's name, vehicle and taxi registrations, owner's initials and religious symbols are also featured.

TRANSPORT

The subcontinent's ubiquitous three-wheel scooter rickshaw is at its most decorative in the South Indian Tamil cities of Mysore and Madurai.

22

TRANSPORT

MADURAI. SOUTH
1157
97
FORHIRE

23
TRANSPORT

COMICS

Detail from one of the numerous comic stalls lining the streets around Churchgate transport centre, Mumbai (Bombay).

24

Earth women depicted as victim and victor of comic-cover extraterrestials in Indian science-fiction stories.

26
COMICS

राज
कॉमिक्स डाइजेस्ट
मूल्य 12.00 संख्या 21

कुबड़ा राजकुमार

STUDIO KADAM

Graphic cartoon
violence on traditional,
contemporary and futuristic
comic-book covers.

29
COMICS

CIRCUS & CINEMA

Cut-out characters promoting a Tamil comedy film in Madurai.

Detail of a
performance
portrayed outside
a Tamil Nadu
roadside circus.

32

CIRCUS & CINEMA

Dramatic highlights of a
performance featuring an
indigenous black panther
are painted around entrance
panels of an itinerant South
Indian circus. Tamil Nadu.

Discarded circus
hoarding on an
abandoned site in
Chennai (formerly
Madras).

34

CIRCUS & CINEMA

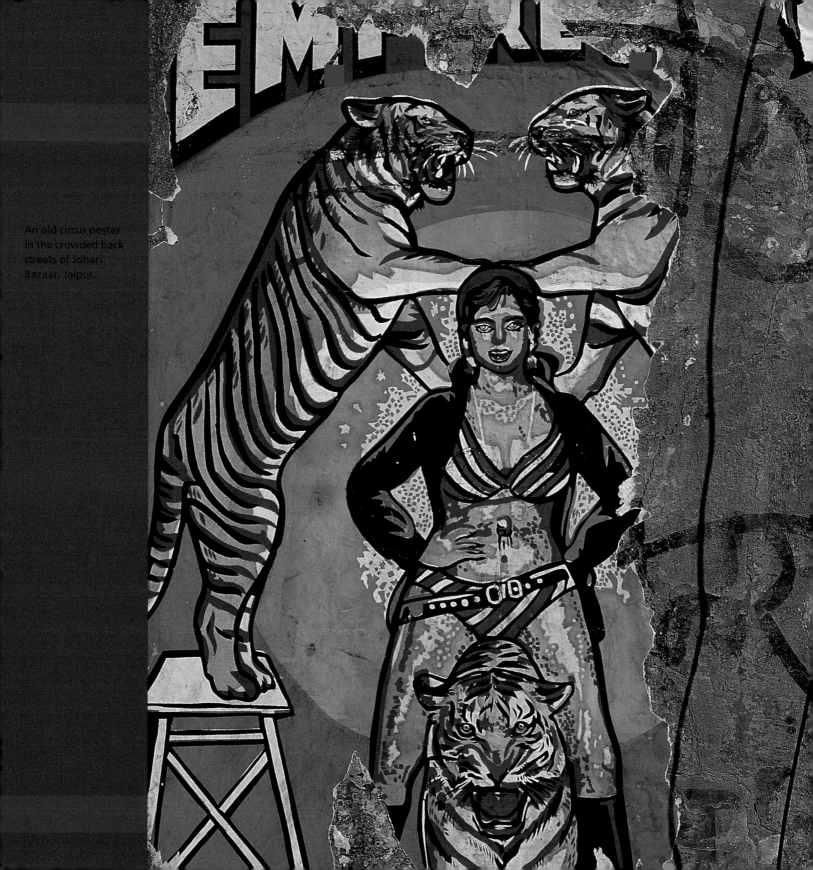

An old circus poster in the crowded back streets of Johari Bazaar, Jaipur.

Comedy duos with regulation sunglasses are big on the streets and in the cinemas of Madurai and Chennai (Madras). Large hoardings line the main streets, on the sides and tops of buildings and in between them.

Hand-painted images are often decorated with three-dimensional stars, garlands and beads, and feature reflective typography in stamped-out adhesive vinyl.

The state of Tamil Nadu produces Tamil-language films that enjoy a regional prominence evident in the giant plywood cut-out promotions along Madurai's streets.

38
CIRCUS & CINEMA

Film posters with religious themes from the *Mahabharata* and *Ramayana*. These two epic tales of Hindu mythology span cinema, comics, theatre, television and advertising.

40 CIRCUS & CINEMA

Jaipur cinemas showing *masala* movies, the popular multiple-genre Hindi film formula from Mumbai, the world's largest film producer and known as 'Bollywood' (from its former name, Bombay).

This week's hit Bollywood comedy movie *Mr. & Mrs. Khiladi* puts bums on seats and bikes in the parking lot. The following week, Hollywood blockbuster *Jurassic Park* repeats the success at the same cinema.

CIRCUS & CINEMA

Traditional rural bandits are replaced by modern Bombay gangsters in Bollywood's new action movies, loosely based on India's changing crime patterns.

A film-set invitation outside Chennai (Madras) airport awaiting the arrival of Queen Elizabeth II during the 1997 Royal visit.

44
CIRCUS & CINEMA

Vigorously brushworked characters from a film on a popular Bollywood theme: betrayal.

Violent revenge is a perennial favourite, and promotion hoardings are painted passionately with a full palette. Highly individual styles have developed in this genre of cinema painting and can be seen in virtual competition on overlapping hoardings in most Indian cities.

Advertising of controversial sex films is heavily censored in India. Censorship is executed on-site with varying degrees of subtlety and creativity, including the use of less controversial posters, a large black brush or discreetly painted additional lingerie.

V.F.D. PRESENTS

THE FILM TELLS ALL THE
SECRETS OF SEX

HIGH HEEL
GIRLS

DIRECTED
AUDE CHABROL

47

CIRCUS & CINEMA

SCULPTURE
& MURALS

Countless thousands of painted stucco images cover Madurai's temple complex, seen here through a wrought-iron screen representing the Hindu deity Lakshmi, goddess of wealth and prosperity.

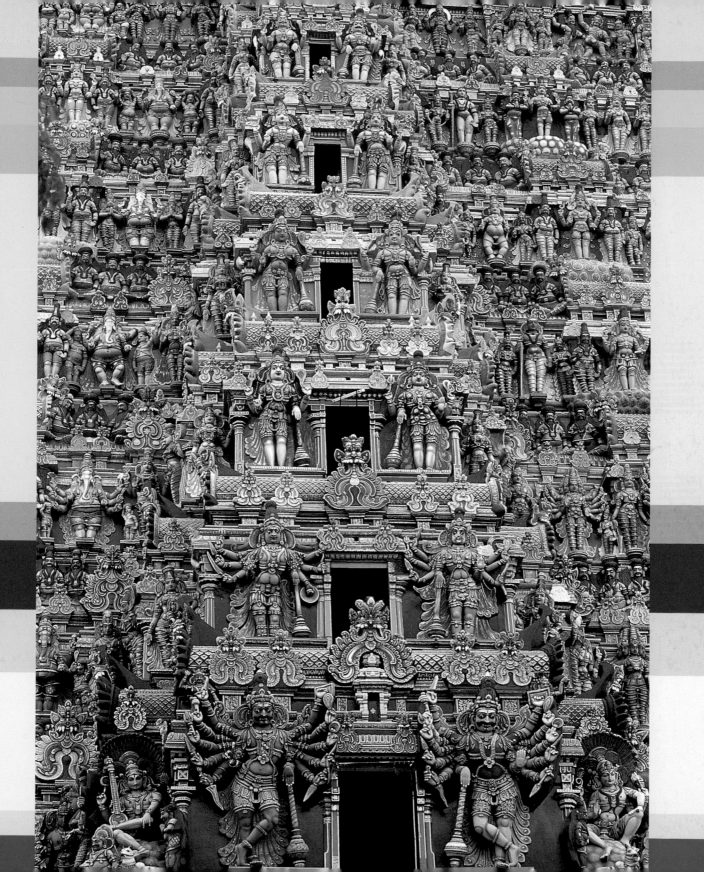

Architectural detail on the King of Puri's house overlooking the holy city's main street, Grand Avenue.

50
SCULPTURE & MURALS

The lone marble occupant of an empty marble building in Jaipur's commercial centre.

Painted stucco and carved wood
façade of a Swami Narayan temple
entrance in Ahmedabad, Gujarat.

51

SCULPTURE & MURALS

Madurai temple fertility effigy covered with offerings from married women seeking divine help with pregnancy.

A roadside shrine of painted stone, representing Lord Rama, is garlanded by worshippers.

A temporary shrine constructed from palm fronds and other found material in Mumbai's business centre. It is attended by a Sadhu with pierced skin, indicating spiritual devotion over material concern.

Details from Christian churches in the former Portuguese colony of Goa include skull-and-crossbones motifs.

54
SCULPTURE & MURALS

Christian martyr
Saint Sebastian
depicted in an
illuminated shrine
in the old spice-
trade port of Fort
Cochin, Kerala.

Theme-park entrance
dinosaurs and cut-out
fashion figures in South
India.

A cluttered junction
of juxtaposed images
in Ernakulam city
centre, Kerala.

56

SCULPTURE & MURALS

A painted stucco effigy of Lord Rama cradles a loudspeaker broadcasting prayers through a temple public address system in Chennai (Madras).

58
SCULPTURE & MURALS

Painted dome of a small tower (*chhatri*) by a water tank in Rajasthan's desert region of Shekhawati. The paintings illustrate Hindu religious stories from the life of Lord Krishna and the *Ramayana*, an epic tale of the Hindu gods, creation and destruction.

Image representing Lord Jagannath, the principal deity of India's holy city
Puri in the eastern state of Orissa. Always portrayed with large eyes and
stumped limbs, Jagannath is depicted sitting on a lotus flower in this
house wall painting.

59

SCULPTURE & MURALS

Early 20th-century European-influenced wall paintings on Shekhawati merchants' *havelis*.

European inventions illustrate the merchant owners' affluence through travel and acquisition.

61

SCULPTURE & MURALS

FASHION

New Delhi women with *mendhi* designs freshly painted on their hands.

Denim fashionwear hoarding in Jaipur's new city. Such blatant sexual metaphors remain hotly debated.

FASHION

Casual, classic
and smart, images
reflecting the change
in India's renowned
textile tradition.

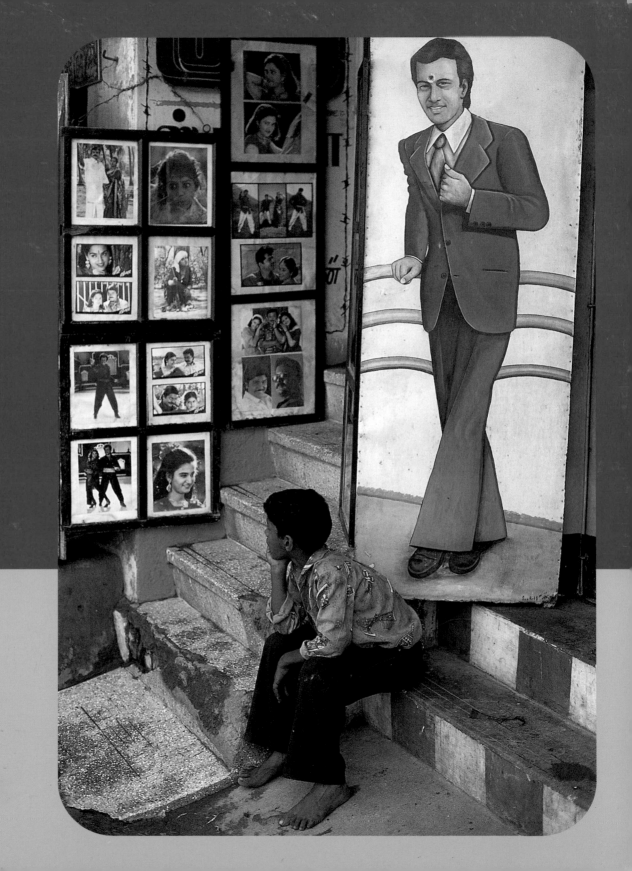

Competing signs obscure the form
of a building housing eleven
tailors' shops in a Madurai suburb.

FASHION

FASHION

Shirt advertisement painted
on a shop wall in Chennai
(Madras).

Steel security roller doors effectively used for advertising by a Madurai military outfitters and fashion tailors when closed for business.

Colour, angular styling and full figure with detail on a Madurai tailor's wall and shutter door.

69
FASHION

Sunday closing of Ernakulam's jewelry shops turns the city's commercial streets into galleries of painted shutters. Jewelry is essential, rather than accessory, in India – not only as a decorative symbol of riches and status, but as a traditional signifier of caste or tribe and also often the portable wealth of nomadic Indians. Jewelry remains a significant part of all Indian marriage dowries.

Mendhi, a dye extract of the henna plant applied to the skin through a pointed plastic bag. These traditional designs stain the skin for several weeks after the dried vegetable pulp is washed off, and are popular with women and girls for fun and celebrations.

LEFT AND RIGHT: Freshly applied henna-pulp designs in the North Indian capital, New Delhi.

BELOW: South Indian *mendhi* designs staining the hands to mark a marital engagement.

FASHION

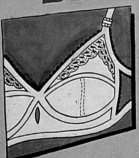

RUPA ®
Softline
BRA.PANTIES

STOCKIST **RAMBALARAM** LUGAPAT (PURI)

M.L.Adv.
PTNA-8
D-7-7-96

®

TS
CKS

VEST   UNDERWEAR   PANTIES

75

FASHION

FASHION

A Bengali village wall used for traditional drying of buffalo-dung fuel pats is also desirable space for fashion advertising.

Designer vandalism or wear and tear? Underwear advertisement on a desert road in Rajasthan.

Wig stalls at the exit from
10th-century Tirumala's Shri
Venkateshvara temple in Andhra
Pradesh. The temple attracts
more pilgrims than Rome or
Mecca and extensive revenue
through donations. Pilgrims
have their heads shaved as an
act of devotion by barbers at
the temple entrance.

SIGNS & ADVERTISING

The signwriter 'Having a Break' is a dummy in this New Delhi promotion of a western product. The image is taken from western advertising concepts, associating handcraft skills with product quality, the irony being that most Indian street advertising, including this, is handcrafted anyway.

A VEIW OF SHOPPING OF POTS FOR DRINKING WATER AT QUEERSCENE TO THE FOREIGN TOURIST

NATHULAL KUMAWAT (INDIA)

953, CHAURA RASTA, JAIPUR-302003, RAJASTHAN

A well-known landmark in Jaipur's old city is the curious potter's shop and its even 'curiouser' sign.

SIGNS & ADVERTISING

Sign outside a watchmaker's shop in Quillon, Kerala.

REAL WATCH WORKS

COMPLAINTS
ABOUT ELEPHANTS
TO BE MADE HERE →
TOURIST OFFICE, AMBER Ph.530264

Associated with elephant-headed god Lord Ganesh, elephants are painted with reverence.

SILENCE ZONE

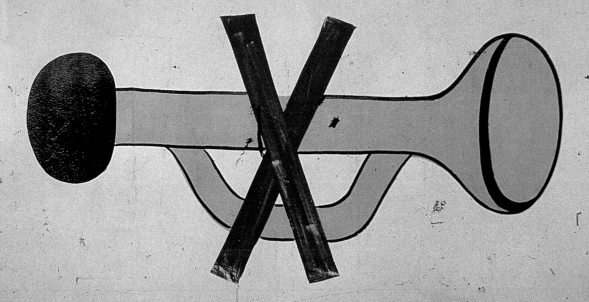

NO HORN PLEASE

A sign outside the
Maharaja of Jaipur's City
Palace, one of the busiest
tourist centres in India.

A fleeing figure indicates the fallibility of safety crossings on India's roads.

SIGNS & ADVERTISING

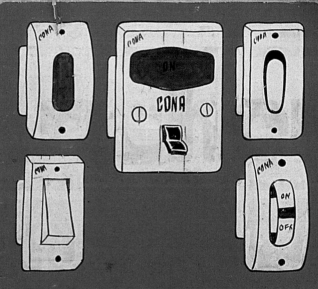

SIGNS & ADVERTISING

Defective electrics unintentionally incorporated in wall advertising for electrical products on commercial buildings in Rajasthan.

MODERN BATHROOM & LATRINE

Public bathrooms for city dwellers and visiting pilgrims without access to piped water or tube wells.

RIGHT: Modesty, portrayed through the use of underwear, is a prerequisite of public bathing in India.

SIGNS & ADVERTISING

BATHROOM & LATRINE

किर गेपार ग्राम

पाखाव क्लौसलय

നവീനകൈവെസ കലിഷ്വ

ബാത്ത് ഉം

SIGNS & ADVERTISING

Western and Indian soft drinks advertising in coastal Goa; in the capital, New Delhi; and in Chennai (formerly Madras).

SIGNS & ADVERTISING

Nothing can match the powers of Puf

Puf

HE IS NOT
SUPERMAN,
BATMAN,
OR POPEYE.
HE IS...

Campaign superheros promoting refrigerators and Doordarshan, India's national television station, in the desert state of Rajasthan.

PACKAGING & DISPLAY

Boxed fireworks on sale in Old Delhi's famous Chandni Chowk bazaar during Diwali, the October/November festival of lights.

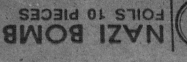

NAZI BOMB
FOILS 10 PIECES

CORONATION'S ®
NAZI
UNBEATABLE

THE CORONATION FIREWORKS
FACTORY. SIVAKASI.

GORONATION FIREWORKS,
M.F. Dt.3/87, 112, East Car Street, SIVAKASI.
EXP. Dt.8/99.Max Retail Price Rs. 86.85 (inclusive of all Taxes)

WARNING:- FLAMMABLE. EXPLODE WITH LOUD SOUND. PLACE
ON LEVEL OPEN SURFACE & GET AWAY. DO NOT HOLD IN
HAND. DON'T FIRE NEAR CHILDREN, OLD & SICK PERSONS. FOR
OUTDOOR USE AND UNDER ADULT SUPERVISION

A combination of word and image
crudely promotes the powerful
shock value of 'Nazi Bomb'
fireworks.

Printed packaging of ice-
cream cones. Rajasthan.

99

PACKAGING & DISPLAY

PACKAGING & DISPLAY

Street stalls arranged with
brightly coloured plastic hair
accessories and children's
toys. Puri, Orissa.

POLITICS

102

Bengali villagers express party support by painting political symbols on the walls of their houses.

Utopian symbolism used in promotion of a prominent Tamil Nadu government minister.

105
POLITICS

Political protest simply but graphically rendered on a wall in the port of Chennai (Madras).

Combined symbols of India's
longest-ruling government party,
the hand of Congress (I), and
colours of the Indian flag suggest
national unity on Bengali village
wall paintings.

सिगरेट हो या शोर अभिशाप है प्रदूष

इंडियन अस्थ

धूआं-धूम्रपान मौत का पैगाम

पर्यावरण यूक्त-नशा मूक्त हो संसार

इण्डियन अस्थमा केयर सोसायटी

110

POLITICS

Pollution in Indian cities is an
increasingly debated political
issue, with hoardings
graphically illustrating its
effect on public health.
Rajasthan.

राबत प्रोपर्टी एण्ड कन्शट्रक्शन

सि
द्धि
सि
मे
न्ट

सि
द्धि
सि
मे
न्ट

53
गे

सॉलिड फायदा

The clenched fist is effectively
used here to advertise industrial
power. Rajasthan.

POLITICS

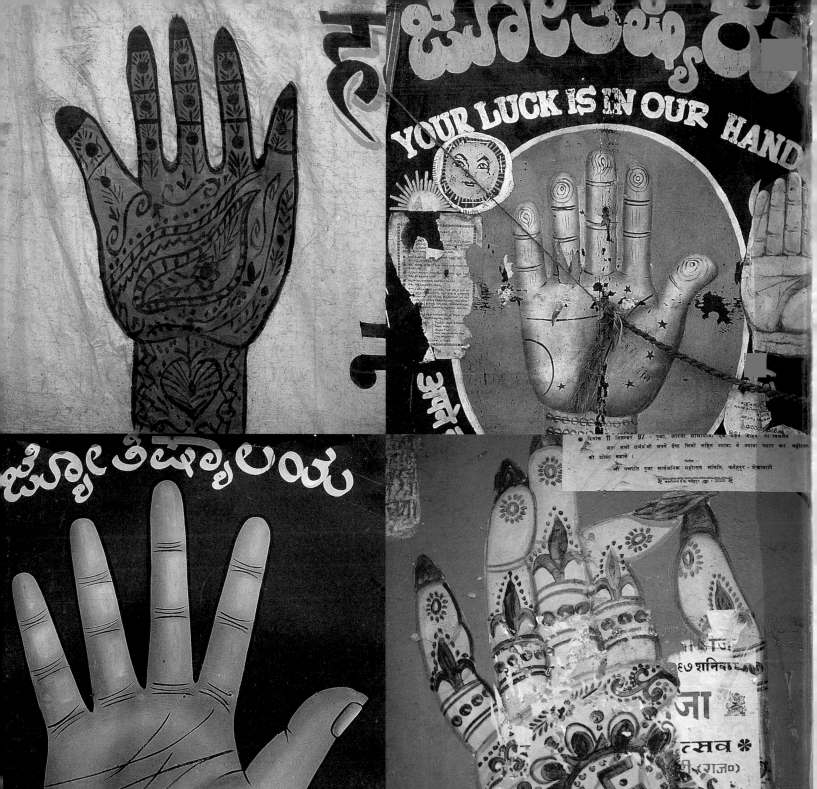